John is Not Afraid

Series: In Father's Footsteps

John is Not Afraid

by

Cor Van Rijswijk

INHERITANCE PUBLICATIONS
NEERLANDIA, ALBERTA, CANADA
PELLA, IOWA, U.S.A.

National Library of Canada Cataloguing in Publication

Rijswijk, Cor van, 1939-
    John is not afraid / by Cor van Rijswijk ; illustrated by Jaap Kramer.

(In father's footsteps)
ISBN 1-894666-81-X

    1. Knox, John, ca. 1514-1572—Juvenile literature. 2. Reformation—
Scotland—Biography—Juvenile literature.
    I. Kramer, Jaap II. Title. III. Series.
BX9223.R53 2004   j285'.2'092   C2004-901588-5

Library of Congress Cataloging-in-Publication Data

Rijswijk, Cor van, 1939-
    [John is niet bang. English]
    John is not afraid / by Cor van Rijswijk.
        p. cm. — (In Father's footsteps)
    ISBN 1-894666-81-X (cloth)
    1. Knox, John, ca. 1514-1572—Juvenile literature. 2. Reformation—
Scotland—Biography—Juvenile literature. I. Title.
BX9223.R5413 2004
285'.2'092—dc22

                                                                    2004003779

Originally published as *John is niet bang* (1993)
by Uitgeverij/Boekhandel Gebr. Koster, Barneveld, The Netherlands
Published with permission.

Translated by Fraser McAdam

Cover Painting and Illustrations by Jaap Kramer

Contents

Chapter   Page

1. Father is Happy 7
2. The Big Book 9
3. Who is Right? 12
4. John Asks Advice 14
5. My Friends, I Am So Glad 17
6. The Lord Speaks 20
7. Minister of the Castle Church 23
8. Caught 25
9. "Come On, Row!" 27
10. John Gets Angry 30
11. Do You See That Tower? 32
12. Free Again! 35
13. John With His Best Friend 37
14. Not Afraid of Anyone 38
15. Farewell 41

Also by
Cor Van Rijswijk:

The Word of the King Series

Abraham's Sacrifice

Gideon Blows the Trumpet

David and Goliath

Audio recordings of these books
are available on Compact Disc.

Dutch titles are also available from

Inheritance Publications
Box 154, Neerlandia, Alberta Canada T0G 1R0
Tel. (780) 674 3949
Web site: http://www.telusplanet.net/public/inhpubl/webip/ip.htm
E-Mail inhpubl@telusplanet.net

1. Father is Happy

John Knox was smart.
He could study very well
and learn quickly.
Father and Mother really liked that.

One day, John was called
to go to his father.
"John," he said,
"you are a big boy now.
You must either work,
or keep going to school."

John looked at his father.
"Father, do you know
what I want to do?
I would like
to become a priest.
That is why I would like
to keep going to school."

Oh, how happy Father was.
Most priests in their country
were very rich.
Now his son would also
become rich and important.
A priest was not only rich
but also very blessed,
because he could work
for the Roman Catholic Church.
He could go to heaven
for all the good works
he had done for the church.

2. The Big Book

John studied hard.
He read a lot,
finishing one book
after another.
He always paid
good attention
to his teachers.

One day he found a big book.
It was written by John Calvin,
who was a very wise man.
But the Roman Catholic Church
did not like John Calvin.
"Calvin is a heretic,"
the priests said.
"He must be put to death!"
Oh, if they could only
get their hands on him,
then he would be
severely punished.
Now John Knox was reading
that big book
by the heretic Calvin.
"What a very good book it is," he thought.
He read it almost every night.
Finally he finished the big book.

"Too bad," sighed John,
"too bad I am finished."
So the next evening
he started reading
the book again.
How wise Calvin was.
He wrote about the Lord,
the children of God,
and the Church of God.
John just couldn't stop reading
the big book.
When he finished reading it
the second time,
he started reading it
for a third time.
Finally he finished it again.
"What a good book this is," John thought.

3. Who is Right?

In that big book
John Calvin wrote about the Bible.
"My dear readers," he wrote,
"I am not bringing a new doctrine
like the priests say.
Indeed not. What I write
you can find in the Bible.
And the Bible
is the Word of God."

John Knox thought about
what he had read
in that big book.
He also prayed to God.
"Lord," he asked,
"Who is right:
the Roman Catholic priests
or John Calvin?"
Many questions arose in his heart.
Was Calvin really a heretic?
Did he have to be killed?
Was he really such a bad man
like the priests said?

4. John Asks Advice

The Lord began to teach John Knox
that John Calvin was not a heretic,
but God's child and servant.
John also came to know the Lord
as Calvin knew Him.
Oh, how John loved the Lord
and His servant Calvin.
He had a strong desire
to meet that man.
It was too bad that he lived
in a land so far away.

John talked about Calvin
with his friends.
It became clear that his teacher,
a professor,
did not like
the Roman Catholic Church either.
"Ah, my boy," he said,
"our priests are rich,
but the Lord Jesus was poor.
He healed the blind
and the crippled.
He did so much good!

But our priests
only think of themselves.
I do not believe that the Pope
can be the head of the church.
Yes, my boy, our Roman Catholic Church
has a lot of errors."

John thought seriously
about what his teacher told him.
Most of all he thought a lot
about Calvin's book.
"I am going to keep
reading that book,"
John thought.
And that was what he did.
Even when he was a priest,
he still read that big book.
He also read a lot in the Bible,
the Word of God.
More and more John saw
the many errors
of the Roman Catholic Church.
There were many things
that were against
the Word of the Lord!

5. My Friends, I Am So Glad

Standing tied to a post
stood a man.
He was wearing a black coat.
That was required by
the Roman Catholic Church.
Now everyone could see
that he was a heretic.
All around him lay wood and straw.
A bag of gunpowder hung
around his neck.
Then the wood and straw
were put on fire.
The flames rose higher and higher.
The man tied to the post
was in great pain,
but still he spoke to the people.

"My friends, I am so glad.
I am so glad that I may suffer
for the Lord Jesus and His Word.
Soon I will sit
at the marriage supper of the Lamb.
Do not listen to the priests
of the Roman Catholic Church.
Only listen to God's Word."

The martyr folded his hands
and lifted his eyes toward heaven.
He prayed, "Father,
into Thy hands
I commend my spirit."

Then it became quiet.
The flames crackled.
The gunpowder exploded.
Still the man was not dead.

6. The Lord Speaks

In the window
of a castle nearby
sat an evil man.
He smiled.
He was enjoying himself.
That man was a good friend
of the Pope,
but a bitter enemy
of the Lord and His servants.

How glad he was
that this heretic was being burned.
"This is going good," he thought,
with a cruel smile on his face.
But suddenly he got a scare.

The martyr looked toward
him and cried,
"You laugh about me now,
but within a few days
you will be lying dead
in that window."

Shortly after this the martyr was taken
to the eternal House of the Father.
His friends wept.
John Knox, his best friend, also wept.
But his enemies were glad.
"Away with those wicked heretics!"
they shouted.

But God stood up for the martyr.
A few days later
the people saw that mocking enemy
lying dead in the window.
That was the punishment he deserved.
The Lord had spoken!

7. Minister of the Castle Church

How dangerous it was for
John and all of God's children.
"Away with those wicked heretics,
and especially with that John Knox!"
the Roman Catholics shouted.
But John just ignored those people.
He knew that the Lord was with him.

Fortunately he was safe now,
safe in a big castle.
Near the castle stood a little church.
There John would speak to the people
about the Lord Jesus.
More and more people
came to listen to him.
One day they asked him something.
"Will you become our minister?"
they asked eagerly.
At first John wanted to say "No."
But the Lord wanted him to say "Yes."
So he told the people,
"Yes, I will become your minister."
Tears were trickling down his cheeks.
"Lord," he wept softly,
"help me, otherwise I cannot
be a good minister."

So John became the minister
of the castle church.

Many people came to the church
to listen to him.
John warned them against
the teaching of the Pope
and of the priests.
"Listen, O people!
Only in the Bible
can you find the truth.
In it you can read
how the Lord wants to be served.
Read that Word often."

8. Caught

Boom! Boom! Boom! Boom!
Large cannonballs were smashing
against the castle walls.
"We will get those heretics,"
the soldiers shouted.
Boom! Boom! Boom! Boom!

John and his friends
heard the cannonballs.
"Lord, help us," they cried.
Frightened, they walked through
the dark halls of the strong castle.
They had nowhere to go.
After a while there was
no food anymore either.
The evil soldiers
were all around the castle
and the city.
Then a terrible sickness broke out.
Hardly anyone could still fight against
the soldiers.
Look, the soldiers
were already entering the city.
Quickly they ran toward the castle.
They especially wanted to get that minister.
He was the worst heretic of all.

9. "Come On, Row!"

Look at them sitting there,
eight men to a bench.
They were rowing very fast,
yet once in a while the whip
cracked above their heads.
"Faster, faster!" commanded
the angry overseer.
There was no way of escape.
They were fastened with chains
to the bench.
They even had to eat
and sleep there.

Once in a while a chain was loosened.
But that was only when a rower had died.
He would just be thrown into the sea.
After all, he was only a slave.
A while later another man
would be forced to sit in his place.

The whip cracked again
against their bent backs.
"Come on, row!" commanded
the strict overseer.
"You too, you nasty heretic!"
he snarled at John Knox.

John rowed day after day.
Weeks and months passed by.
How tired and weak he became.
This work was too heavy for him.
While rowing he silently
prayed to God,
asking the Lord to rescue him.
He knew that the Lord saw him there.
Would the Lord hear him?

10. John Gets Angry

A man climbed down into the ship.
He was holding a picture in his hand,
a portrait of a woman.
"This is the holy mother,"
said the Roman Catholic man.
He showed John the picture.
"Kiss the holy mother,"
the man said to John.
But John became angry.
Do you think he would do that?
He did not want to kiss
and honour a picture.
He took the portrait
and threw it into the water.
"Away with it!" he said.
"There is only one Holy One,
and that is the Lord Jesus Christ!"

How angry that Roman Catholic man was!
"You just wait, heretic!
We will get you yet!" he yelled.

11. Do You See That Tower?

One day John became very ill.
Yet he still had to row.
Once in a while the whip cracked.
Swish-swoosh, swish-swoosh.
"Keep rowing, heretic!"
called the strict overseer.

But John could barely keep going.
The other rowers could see
how the poor minister was suffering.
"Oh, now he will soon die,"
they thought.
John peered outside through the window.
Suddenly he sat up straight.
His dull eyes began
to sparkle with happiness.
"Look, do you see
that tower in the distance?
It is by the castle!
That is where I first preached,
and the Lord will bring me back there.
Yes, that is what He will do!
I know it for sure!"
How John shouted for joy!
The other rowers also
looked through the window.

Yes, in the distance they also
could see the tower and the castle.
But would John really preach there again?
Would he be set free?

12. Free Again!

Clank-clank! Clank-clank!
John's chains fell off.
"Come along," said the overseer.
"You may go. You are free!"

A while later
a happy man walked
through the streets.
Once in a while
he would lift up his eyes.
"Lord, Thou hast given me
my freedom again,"
he said thankfully.
Now he could preach again.
Not long after this
he preached in the little church,
whose tower he had seen
while he was sitting
on that hard rowing-bench.

13. John With His Best Friend

John was still not left alone.
The Roman Catholics
kept bothering him.
Because he was persecuted
in his own country
he fled to a far-away country.
There he was going to live
near his best friend, John Calvin.
Oh, he really liked living there.
"Calvin's church is
the Church of the Lord Jesus,"
he said happily.
The two friends talked often
about the Lord and His Church.

14. Not Afraid of Anyone

Yet John longed
for his own country.
At last he returned
to his fatherland.
God's children were very happy!
"Reverend Knox, you should stay
with us for always now," they said.

John preached often,
sometimes twice a day.

Many people left the church of Rome
and very many people were
converted to the Lord.
The Roman Catholics were angry with John,
especially the Roman Catholic queen.
She wanted the whole country
to become Roman Catholic.
"Reverend, stop preaching!"
she threatened.
But John did not listen.
He only listened to the Lord
and continued preaching.
He even had to go to the palace
more than once.

39

"Why don't you listen?"
the queen asked angrily.
"Your Majesty, I fear the Lord.
He wants me to preach,
and therefore I continue,"
answered the brave minister.

That was how John Knox preached
throughout the whole land.
It seemed as though
he was not afraid of anyone.
The enemy wanted to kill him.
But still John preached on.
"My life is in God's hands," he said.

For many years,
he pointed out the way of salvation
to the people of his land.

15. Farewell

Now John was old.
He felt that he was becoming weaker.
Sometimes strong men
had to help him get into the pulpit.

The last Sunday he preached,
he spoke about the death
of the Lord Jesus,
his dear Saviour.
John knew: "The Lord Jesus
also died for me,
and therefore I will go
to be with Him in heaven."
How great was his desire
to be with Christ eternally.

After the sermon,
he walked home,
leaning on a cane.
Many people had waited for him.
They had shaken his hand
and said goodbye to him.
"Goodbye, Reverend," they wept.
Oh, they loved him so much.
How they would miss him.

Several weeks later John lay dying.
Often he lifted his hands
toward heaven.
How he was longing to die.
"Now I will soon be
with the Lord," he sighed.
Many times his friends
read to him from the Bible.

Gladly he would say,
"What a beautiful chapter that was."
Now he knew that he
would leave the earth
within a short time.

A little later he prayed,
"Lord, into Thy hands
I commend my spirit."
This was his last prayer.
He lifted his hands upward,
sighed twice,
and breathed his last breath.

And so John Knox
departed joyfully
to his Father's House.

1. A Great Miracle

Abraham was rich.
He had many cows and sheep,
donkeys and camels.
He also had lots
of gold and silver.
The LORD had given him
all these animals
and things.

Abraham also had a child.
His name was Isaac.
Oh, Abraham
loved him very much.
He had also received
that child from the LORD.

The Word of the King Series

Abraham's
Sacrifice

Cor Van Rijswijk
Illustrated by Rino Visser

Abraham's Sacrifice
by Cor Van Rijswijk
Time: Abraham   Age: 4-8
ISBN 1-894666-21-6
Can.$8.95 U.S.$7.90

1. There They Come Again

"Flee!
We must flee!
There they come again!"
Full of fear
the people ran away.
Mothers snatched
up their children
and ran away too.

Soon there was
no one in sight;
everyone was in hiding.
Many of the people
hid in caves.

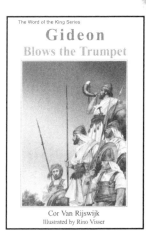

1. Looking for David

Through the fields
walked a man.
He was looking around,
searching here
and searching there.
Was he looking
for someone?

From time to time
he would cry out:
"David! David!"
Then he would
look around again.
He gazed
into the distance.
"Where can
that boy be?"
he wondered aloud.

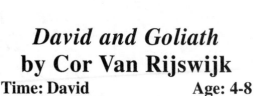

David and Goliath
by Cor Van Rijswijk
Time: David   Age: 4-8
ISBN 1-894666-23-2
    Can.$8.95 U.S.$7.90

The Word of the King Series

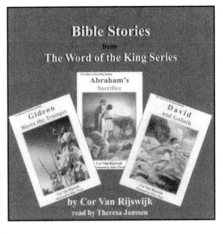

These hard-cover Bible story books are wonderful. Children just learning to read can use them as little readers, either reading them on their own, reading them aloud, or reading them along with the narration on CD. Yet what every child enjoys most is being read to. Here are Bible stories written in language which is simple and reverent. These are stories which edify both adults and children. The drawings must also be given due attention: they are simply beautiful. Real to life, they are a great contrast to the modern concept of Bible cartoon characters. There is a great need for good reading for children. Here is a good beginning.

Rev. J. Visscher in *Clarion*: "These books are usually about 40 pages long, are well-illustrated by Rino Visser and are faithful, biblical renderings. They make for good birthday presents to four and five year olds."

BIBLE STORIES
for our little ones

by

W.G. VAN DE HULST

Illustrated
by J.H. Isings

This book is intended to be a book for mothers. A book to be read in quiet hours, to little ones of four to seven or eight years old who sit at Mother's knee. A book to be read slowly yes, especially slowly; very clearly with warm, loving reverence and awe which creates in little children s heart a pious reverence and a joy filled awe. It desires to be a BIBLE FOR THE LITTLE ONES, reaching out to all areas of a child s understanding. A child does not comprehend everything, yet understands a great deal. This story bible wishes to tell about the holy things in plain, clear, almost simple language, which still must never profane the consecrated happenings. It is not meant to be complete. Completeness would hinder children. This book is not meant to be anything but a modest, reverent endeavour to lead the little ones into the holy sphere of Godly things. The interest of the little ones will be the test to see whether this endeavour is accomplished. May God give our little ones His wonderful blessings in the quiet hours, listening to His voice at Mother's knee.

— The Author

Subject: Bible   **Age: 7-10**
ISBN 1-894666-69-0   **Can.$29.95 U.S.$24.90**